THE
Archive Photographs
SERIES

P&A CAMPBELL
PLEASURE STEAMERS
FROM 1946

The flagship of the White Funnel Fleet from 1946 to 1968, the *Bristol Queen*, passes beneath the Clifton Suspension Bridge on Wednesday 2 September 1964.

THE
Archive Photographs
SERIES

P&A CAMPBELL
PLEASURE STEAMERS
FROM 1946

Compiled by
Chris Collard

TEMPUS

Tempus Publishing Limited
The Mill, Brimscombe Port,
Stroud, Gloucestershire, GL5 2QG

ISBN 0 7524 1722 3

Typesetting and origination by
Tempus Publishing Limited
Printed in Great Britain by
Midway Clark Printing, Wiltshire

Acknowledgements

The photographs which appear in this book are taken from my collection which has been assembled over many years from a wide variety of sources. Most of those taken from 1960 are from my own camera. It is impossible to acknowledge the origin of every illustration but I wish to express my gratitude to the late H.A. Allen, the late Ernest Dumbleton, the late Edwin Keen, and the late Graham Langmuir. My good friends Dr Donald Anderson, the Reverend Norman Bird, Mr John Brown, Mr Nigel Coombes, Mr Viv Davies, Mr Sidney Robinson and Mr Lionel Vaughan have been a source of inspiration as well as practical help in allowing me to use their photographs. Once again, Mr George Owen, the doyen of Bristol Channel historians, has been of invaluable assistance in checking my manuscript in pursuit of historical accuracy.

Contents

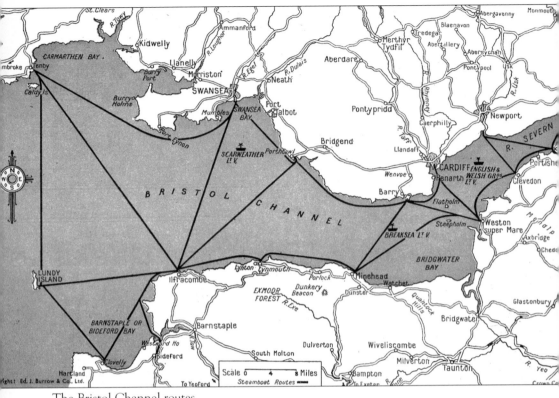

The Bristol Channel routes.

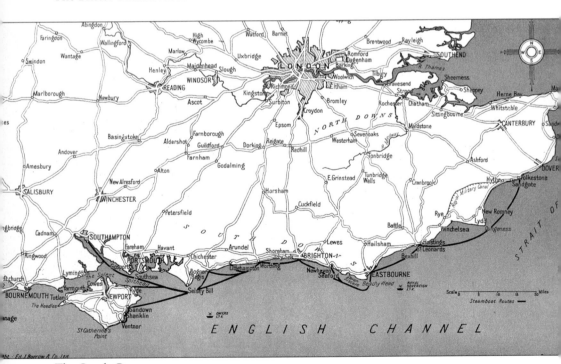

The South Coast routes.

Introduction

The paddle steamers of P&A Campbell's White Funnel Fleet plied the waters of the Bristol Channel for over seventy years. The company's origins lie in early nineteenth century Scotland where the Campbell family began its steamer services on the River Clyde. In the 1880s a series of events resulted in the Campbell brothers, Peter and Alexander, transferring their business from Glasgow to Bristol, where, despite intense competition, they quickly established themselves as the major pleasure steamer operators. As the popularity of marine excursions flourished in the 1890s, they increased the size of their fleet, extending their network of Bristol Channel services and venturing into a new enterprise on the South Coast.

The Golden Age of the paddle steamer ended abruptly with the outbreak of the First World War when, in common with most other fleets, the thirteen Campbell vessels were requisitioned by the Admiralty for minesweeping purposes.

At the end of the hostilities the company recommenced its peace-time services which continued through the difficult years of industrial unrest, the Depression and impending conflict, until the declaration of the Second World War, when the Admiralty, once again, requisitioned the entire fleet.

Of the eleven paddle steamers which took part in the Second World War, only four returned to civilian service – the *Ravenswood*, *Britannia*, *Glen Usk* and *Glen Gower*. They were joined by the turbine steamer, *Empress Queen*, which had been requisitioned by the Admiralty immediately after completion of her trials in 1940, and by two new paddle steamers, the *Bristol Queen*, in 1946, and the *Cardiff Queen*, in 1947.

The post-war sailings began in April 1946 and, for the 1946 and the following three seasons, the company enjoyed profitable summers with passenger figures reaching pre-war proportions. The situation, however, changed drastically in the 1950s, when the company embarked upon what was to become an heroic struggle against overwhelming odds.

The weather during the 1950 season was atrocious. Many trips were cancelled or curtailed, and additional expenses were incurred by having to accommodate stranded passengers overnight and returning them home by alternative transport. Furthermore, the de-rationing of petrol after ten years and the greater financial accessibility of the motor car, led to a considerable rise in private motoring and a general trend from excursion steamer travel.

The next four seasons followed a similar pattern, but the summer of 1955 took a turn for the better and, for the first time since 1949, the company made a profit. Unfortunately it was too late. The combination of the previous years' losses, the maintenance of ageing ships and rising fuel costs conspired to present a bleak prospect for the company's future.

Ships were gradually withdrawn from service and broken up. Further bad summers followed and, at the end of 1958, the company was placed in the hands of a receiver. However, two steamers entered service for the 1959 season in an attempt to resuscitate the company's fortunes. A good summer followed and, at the end of the year, it was announced that P&A Campbell Ltd had been taken over by the financiers George Nott Industries Ltd.

The early 1960s marked the beginning of an 'Indian Summer' for the company. However, the two surviving paddle steamers, the *Cardiff Queen* and *Bristol Queen*, were a considerable drain on the company's resources being big ships to fill and costly to run. The 'last straw' was the opening of the Severn Bridge in August 1966, which had an adverse effect on the Cardiff-to-Weston ferry – the mainstay of the company's operations. Ultimately, the harsh realities of economics caused the demise of the two *Queens* after their tragically short lives. They went to the breaker's yard in the spring of 1968, bringing to an end the long line of paddle steamers which had graced the waters of the Bristol Channel for so long.

During the 1960s the company purchased three motor vessels, the *St Trillo*, the *Vecta*, (renamed *Westward Ho*), and the *Balmoral*. Their economy of operation made them more financially viable, but the ships themselves lacked the charisma of the paddle steamers. Gone were the spacious decks, the reassuring rhythmic beat of the paddles and the hypnotic fascination of watching the engines in motion. Nevertheless, the company continued its services until the end of the 1980 season. In the following year the *Balmoral* was sold and P&A Campbell Ltd finally passed into history. It appeared that the tradition which the Campbell brothers had started nearly one hundred years before had ended – but not quite!

In 1973 the last sea-going paddle steamer in the world, the Glasgow-based *Waverley*, was withdrawn from her River Clyde services. She was sold by her owners, Caledonian MacBrayne Ltd, to a company formed by the Paddle Steamer Preservation Society for the sum of £1. Initially, her new owners, Waverley Steam Navigation Co. Ltd, ran her on the River and Firth of Clyde but gradually began to extend her services.

On a fine May evening in 1979 the *Waverley* arrived at Penarth Pier to make the first of her Bristol Channel sailings. It was a tentative beginning which lasted for only a few days but it was enough to rekindle a nostalgic enthusiasm for the many passengers who never thought to see a paddle steamer in the Bristol Channel again. During subsequent years the *Waverley* toured the country, making annual visits to the Bristol Channel of about a month duration, running a wide variety of cruises, recalling days gone by and introducing a new generation to the delights of paddle steamer travel.

In 1986 the company purchased the *Balmoral*, then moored in Dundee, following an abortive attempt to use her as a floating restaurant after her sale by P&A Campbell Ltd. With her return to the Bristol Channel the *Balmoral* continued the White Funnel Fleet tradition, and also acted as consort to the *Waverley* on her countrywide journeys. Their sailings continue to this day, and the ships have firmly established themselves as a regular part of the summer scene all around our coast, bringing pleasure to the many passengers who relish sea air and fine scenery, just as their grandparents had done during the paddle steamers' Victorian heyday.

One
The 1940s

Saturday 22 June 1946. The *Britannia* passing Battery Point, Portishead, on her way from Bristol to Cardiff, Penarth, Barry and Ilfracombe.

The *Bristol Queen* about to be launched. The ceremony was performed by the Lady Mayoress of Bristol, using a bottle of Bristol Milk Sherry, which failed to break at the first attempt. The *Bristol Queen* was the largest of all the White Funnel paddle steamers, with a length of 244ft 7ins and gross tonnage of 961.

The *Bristol Queen* launched at Charles Hill's Yard, Bristol, on Thursday 4 April 1946, exactly one year to the day after the contract for her building was signed; a remarkable feat considering the shortages of manpower and materials following the war.

Saturday 13 April 1946. The forty-five year old *Ravenswood* in the River Avon on the first post-war trip, a cruise from Bristol to off Clevedon.

The *Ravenswood* re-commences the sailings from Cardiff with an afternoon trip to Bristol. She is seen leaving the Pier Head on Sunday 14 April 1946.

The *Bristol Queen* fitting out at Hill's Yard, Sunday 23 June 1946. Her design followed the contemporary trend for concealed paddle boxes and the additional shelter of sun lounges on her promenade deck.

Sunday 28 July 1946. The *Bristol Queen* fitting out at Hill's Yard. On the left is the *Glen Gower*, undergoing an extensive post-war refit, with her two funnels lying on the quayside.

The *Britannia* lying at P&A Campbell's Underfall Yard, in the Bristol City Docks, on Sunday 28 July 1946, having been withdrawn from service owing to boiler failure. The floor of her 1935 'Haystack' boiler had collapsed six weeks after she re-entered service, no doubt because of hard running and lack of maintenance during the war years. The cost of its replacement became the subject of negotiations with the Admiralty.

Sunday 4 August 1946. The *Glen Usk* in the River Avon. She had been rushed into service following the laying up of the *Britannia*.

Saturday 7 September 1946. The *Bristol Queen* leaving Bristol for trials.

P. & A. CAMPBELL LTD.

SPECIAL ANNOUNCEMENT

MAIDEN VOYAGE of P.S. BRISTOL QUEEN
SATURDAY, September 14th, 1946
BRISTOL to ILFRACOMBE (Direct)

Leave BRISTOL (Hotwells Landing Stage) 9.15 a.m
Leave ILFRACOMBE 5.15 p.m.   Direct to Bristol

CATERING ON BOARD   FARES : Single 11/- Day Return 14/6

Tickets obtainable on Steamer   No Advance Bookings

T. & W. GOULDING LTD., BRISTOL 1.

The timetable for the *Bristol Queen's* maiden trip.

Saturday 14 September 1946. The *Bristol Queen* leaving Bristol on her maiden trip.

Saturday 14 September 1946. The *Bristol Queen* arriving at Ilfracombe for the first time.

The company's second new post-war paddle steamer under construction at Fairfield's Yard, Glasgow, early in 1947.

The *Cardiff Queen* about to be launched by Mrs Banks, the wife of the company managing director, on Wednesday 26 February 1947. The *Cardiff Queen* was slightly smaller than her sister, with a length of 240ft and gross tonnage of 765.

Last minute preparations take place aboard the *Cardiff Queen* shortly before leaving Glasgow for trials on 12 June 1947.

The *Cardiff Queen* on trials in the Firth of Clyde on 12 June 1947. The average speed attained was $17\frac{1}{2}$ knots – half a knot slower than the builder's guaranteed speed.

The *Cardiff Queen* arriving at Bristol from Glasgow on Thursday 19 June 1947. On her journey south she encountered a south-easterly gale in the Irish Sea and had to shelter overnight in Holyhead.

The *Cardiff Queen* at the Underfall Yard on arrival from the builders, with rust already appearing on her hull. A considerable number of imperfections manifested themselves over subsequent years and the company wrote to Fairfield's in 1952: 'In general the vessel has not reached our expectations of a Clyde built steamer.'

The *Cardiff Queen* arriving at Ilfracombe in 1947.

The *Cardiff Queen* leaving Weston on Saturday 5 July 1947. In the distance the *Glen Usk* waits to berth at the pier.

The turbine steamer *Empress Queen* arriving at Bristol from Troon, after reconditioning by her builders, on Wednesday 18 June 1947. She had been ordered in 1939 and launched in the following year. Immediately after completion, however, she had been requisitioned by the Admiralty, originally to serve as an anti-aircraft ship and later as a troop transport running between Stranraer and Larne.

The *Empress Queen* on her first visit to Ilfracombe on Saturday 28 June 1947. She had been destined for the South Coast primarily to run the continental sailings, but, after the war, Government restrictions effectively suspended such day excursions. The *Empress Queen* was placed on the Swansea-to-Ilfracombe service but was found to be unsuitable as her size and lack of manoeuvrability were causing serious berthing difficulties.

CAMPBELL'S SAILINGS

1947

(WEATHER & CIRCUMSTANCES PERMITTING)

From SWANSEA (South Dock Entrance)

By the new, fast, luxurious, Turbine Twin Screw Steamer

" EMPRESS QUEEN "

JUNE 27th to JULY 7th (inclusive)
For Sailings from PORTHCAWL see Page 3.

FRIDAY, JUNE 27th

7.30 p.m. Evening Cruise around SCARWEATHER LIGHT VESSEL and towards PORTHCAWL. Back about 10 p.m. Fare 5/-.

SATURDAY, JUNE 28th

10.0 a.m. Day trip to ILFRACOMBE. Leave Ilfracombe 8 p.m. for Swansea.

10.0 a.m. Morning Cruise calling at ILFRACOMBE. Back about 2 p.m. Fare 10/-.

2.30 p.m. Afternoon trip to ILFRACOMBE. Leave Ilfracombe 8.0 p.m. for Swansea. Special Fare this trip 10/- Single or Return.

A timetable for the *Empress Queen*'s Swansea sailings. They were cancelled from Monday 7 July after it was decided to send her to the South Coast to replace the *Glen Gower*.

An extract from the *Empress Queen*'s log book showing part of her rough passage to the South Coast.

The *Glen Gower* had entered service from Brighton in May 1947 but returned to the Bristol Channel in July. She is seen here at Ilfracombe on Tuesday 14 August 1947.

Saturday 27 March 1948. The largest and smallest members of the post-war fleet, the *Ravenswood* and *Empress Queen* in the Merchant's Dock, Bristol.

During 1947 the *Britannia* had been re-boilered, at the expense of the Admiralty, with a double-ended boiler necessitating two funnels. She re-entered service in 1948 and is seen in the River Avon returning from boiler trials on 10 May.

The *Britannia* joined the *Empress Queen* on the South Coast for the seasons of 1948 and 1949. The two ships are shown in Newhaven Harbour, with the *Empress Queen* on the gridiron for bottom painting.

The *Glen Usk* at the Landing Stage, Newport, in 1949.

The *Glen Usk* arriving at Weston on a blustery day in the late 1940s.

The *Bristol Queen* at Hotwells Landing Stage, Bristol, on Saturday 4 June 1949.

Under a threatening sky, the *Glen Gower* leaves Swansea for an evening cruise in 1949.

Ilfracombe Pier was in need of considerable repair following the period of wartime neglect. Rebuilding took place during the early 1950s but in this view, taken on 1 September 1949, the builders are in the process of preparatory work. The *Cardiff Queen* arrives, somewhat unusually, 'bow out'.

At Lundy, Lynmouth and Clovelly the passengers were ferried between the ships and the shore by small boats. The *Glen Gower* awaits the re-embarkation of her passengers off Lundy on Wednesday 17 August 1949.

CAMPBELL'S SAILINGS, 1949
(Weather and Circumstances Permitting)

Sept. 17th   Sept. 26th

LAST TRIPS OF THE SEASON
From CLEVEDON PIER

SATURDAY, SEPTEMBER 17th.

1.40 p.m.   **Afternoon Cruise, calling at BRISTOL** (3.15 p.m.). Back about 4.15 p.m. Fare **4/-**.

4.20 p.m.   **Evening Cruise, calling at PENARTH** 5.15 p.m., **CARDIFF** 5.40 p.m. Back about 6.50 p.m. Fare **5/-**.

4.20 p.m.   **Single Trip to PENARTH, CARDIFF, BARRY PIER and ILFRACOMBE.** PLEASE NOTE: Passengers for Barry Pier and Ilfracombe change Steamers at Cardiff, departing from there at 5.50 p.m.

9.45 p.m.   **Single Trip to PENARTH and CARDIFF.** NOTE: A Steamer leaving Ilfracombe at 9.15 a.m., Lynmouth 9.45 a.m., Barry Pier 11.30 a.m., connects with a Steamer leaving Penarth 12 noon, Cardiff 12.30 p.m. for Clevedon. (Passengers change Steamers at Cardiff for Clevedon.)

A booklet timetable for 1949.

At the end of the exceptionally fine and busy summer of 1949, the *Ravenswood, Britannia, Glen Usk* and *Empress Queen* lie at their winter quarters in the Merchant's Dock, Bristol.

28

Two
The 1950s

The *Ravenswood* leaving Weston on a day which epitomises the weather of the 1950 season.

The *Bristol Queen* being painted at the Underfall Yard, Bristol, in the spring of 1950.

The first trip of the season from Swansea. The *Cardiff Queen* leaves for Ilfracombe on Saturday 27 May 1950.

The *Cardiff Queen* and *Empress Queen* at anchor off Ilfracombe on Thursday 22 June 1950. The latter was *en route* from Bristol to Newhaven but was delayed for a short while owing to mechanical problems.

The *Bristol Queen* at Ilfracombe on Saturday 19 August 1950 with reconstruction of the pier well under way.

Above and below: Ilfracombe on a wet and windy day in August 1950. The *Glen Gower* was the only steamer to venture 'down-channel' and is seen coming in from her anchorage to take the return sailing to Newport.

Above and below: The *Ravenswood* leaving Penarth in the early 1950s.

Engine room of the *Cardiff Queen*.

Engine room of the *Bristol Queen*.

The *Bristol Queen* at Barry on her way from Bristol to Ilfracombe on Whit Monday 14 May 1951.

Aboard the *Britannia*, bound for Ilfracombe.

CAMPBELL'S SAILINGS
(Weather and Circumstances Permitting)

MONDAY, AUGUST 13th
TO
TUESDAY, AUGUST 28th
1951

FROM NEWPORT
By P/S "RAVENSWOOD," P/S "GLEN USK" and P/S "GLEN GOWER"

MONDAY, AUGUST 13th
2.30 p.m. **AFTERNOON CRUISE TO OFF CLEVEDON** (3 hours). Fare 4/6.

6 p.m. **SINGLE TRIP TO WESTON AND BARRY.** Fare, Weston or Barry, 5/6.

NOTE.—A Steamer leaves Weston at 1 p.m. for Newport.

TUESDAY, AUGUST 14th
2.30 p.m. **CHANNEL CRUISE up the River Avon, calling at Bristol.** Leave Bristol 5 p.m. for Newport. Fare 5/6.

7.30 p.m. **SINGLE TRIP TO WESTON AND BARRY.** Fare, Weston or Barry, 5/6.

NOTE.—A Steamer leaves Barry at 12 noon and Weston at 1 p.m. for Newport.

WEDNESDAY, AUGUST 15th
NO SAILINGS FROM NEWPORT THIS DAY.

THURSDAY, AUGUST 16th
9 a.m. **DAY TRIP TO WESTON.** Leave Weston 5.30 p.m. for Newport.

7 p.m. **CHANNEL CRUISE to English and Welsh Grounds' Lightship** (2 hours). Fare 4/-.

NOTE.—A Steamer leaves Cardiff at 7.15 a.m. for Newport.

FRIDAY, AUGUST 17th
9.30 a.m. **DAY TRIP TO WESTON.** Leave Weston 8.45 p.m. for Newport.

SATURDAY, AUGUST 18th
9.15 a.m. **DAY TRIP TO WESTON AND PENARTH.** Leave Penarth 6.25 p.m., Weston 7.30 p.m. for Newport.

SUNDAY, AUGUST 19th
9.15 a.m. **DAY TRIP TO WESTON, LYNMOUTH AND ILFRACOMBE.** Leave Ilfracombe 5.45 p.m., Lynmouth 6.15 p.m., Weston 8.30 p.m. for Newport.

MONDAY, AUGUST 20th
9.15 a.m. **DAY TRIP TO WESTON.** Leave Weston 8.45 p.m. for Newport.

TUESDAY, AUGUST 21st
9.30 a.m. **DAY TRIP TO WESTON.** Leave Weston 9 p.m. for Newport.

A timetable for 1951.

Aboard the *Ravenswood* at Clevedon Pier in 1951.

The *Bristol Queen* at Ilfracombe in 1951.

From left to right: the *Bristol Queen*, *Glen Gower*, *Ravenswood* and *Glen Usk* at the Pier Head, Cardiff, in 1951.

A highlight of the 1951 season was the re-opening of Minehead as a port of call. The pier had been demolished, on military orders, during the war, but the harbour was dredged to give sufficient depth of water for the steamers to berth at the jetty. The *Glen Usk* is seen at the opening ceremony, on Saturday 2 June 1951.

The *Empress Queen* at Torquay, 1951. The *Empress Queen*'s four seasons on the Sussex coast had not been a success, partly because berthing at the piers was a slow process, but mainly because she seemed to be impossible to fill with sufficient passengers. Arrangements were made for her to sail from Torquay during the 1951 season, operating a service to the Channel Islands thrice weekly, with coastal cruises on the intervening days. The cross-Channel sailings were relatively successful, an average of 505 passengers being carried per trip, but the coastal cruises were a disaster. She sometimes ran with less than fifty passengers aboard and, in mid-July, such trips were abandoned entirely. During the course of her twelve-week season, forty-two sailing days were lost because of a combination of the aborted coastal cruises, repairs, off-service days and bad weather. With cross-Channel trips to France still out of the question, the company had no alternative other than to lay her up.

The *Empress Queen* laid up at Narrow Quay, Bristol, in 1952.

The 1952 Sussex coast season was maintained by the *Cardiff Queen*, seen here at Newhaven on her arrival from Bristol on Monday 23 June 1952.

Above and below: Aboard the *Glen Gower* crossing from Swansea-to-Ilfracombe in a gale on Saturday 9 August 1952. Although an excellent sea-boat, the very heavy seas forced her to turn back off the Scarweather Lightvessel, about an hour after leaving Swansea.

At the 1953 Coronation Naval Review in Spithead, three of the White Funnel steamers were present: the *Glen Gower* and the two *Queens*. The *Bristol Queen* is shown, above, at Southampton in between her cruises around the fleet, and the *Glen Gower*, below, is seen cruising in Spithead.

The *Glen Gower* leaving Bristol on her first trip of the 1954 season. In 1954 urgent measures were taken in an attempt to reverse the decline in the company's fortunes of the previous four seasons. Further ports of call were re-opened in the Bristol Channel and the *Glen Gower* replaced the *Cardiff Queen* on the South Coast in order to resume the cross-Channel sailings to Boulogne, although passports were essential. (The *Cardiff Queen* was precluded from making such crossings.) Publicity was increased and the timetables became larger and more fully detailed. 1954 was also designated as the company's 'Centenary Year'.

Sailings from

PORTHCAWL
by the Steamers of the
White Funnel Fleet

" BRISTOL QUEEN "
" CARDIFF QUEEN "
" BRITANNIA "

" GLEN GOWER "
" GLEN USK "
" RAVENSWOOD "

CENTENARY YEAR 1854—1954

The first Steamer built for the Campbells, named "Express," sailed on the Clyde in 1854.
The Bristol Channel Service commenced 1887, Limited Company formed 1893

FOR DESCRIPTION OF ROUTES & POINTS OF INTEREST SEE OVERLEAF

SUNDAY, JUNE 20th.	10.30 a.m. 8.45 p.m.	**Day Trip to WESTON** Leave Weston 6.30 p.m. for Porthcawl. **Single Trip to SWANSEA.** Note.—Steamer leaves Swansea 9.30 a.m. for Porthcawl.
MONDAY, JUNE 21st.	10.0 a.m. 10.0 a.m. 10.0 a.m. 8.20 p.m.	**Day Trip to ILFRACOMBE** Leave Ilfracombe 6.40 p.m. for Porthcawl. **Day Trip to ILFRACOMBE and Cruise to PORLOCK BAY** Fare to include Cruise 15s.6d. Passengers for Cruise change Steamers at Ilfracombe in forward direction only. Steamer leaves Ilfracombe for Cruise at 2.45 p.m. **Single Trip to MINEHEAD, LYNMOUTH and ILFRACOMBE.** **Single Trip to BARRY, WESTON, CLEVEDON and BRISTOL.** Note.—Steamer leaves Swansea 9.0 a.m. for Porthcawl.
SUNDAY, JUNE 27th.	2.15 p.m. 4.30 p.m.	**Afternoon Cruise to the SCARWEATHER LIGHTSHIP** Back about 4.15 p.m. Fare 4s. **Single Trip to ILFRACOMBE.** Note.—Steamer leaves Ilfracombe 12.15 p.m. for Porthcawl.
SUNDAY, JULY 4th.	10.55 a.m. 8.50 p.m.	**Day Trip to WESTON** Leave Weston 6.40 p.m. for Porthcawl. **Single Trip to PORT TALBOT and SWANSEA.** Note.—Steamer leaves Swansea 9.30 a.m. Port Talbot 10.15 a.m. for Porthcawl.
MONDAY, JULY 5th.	10.0 a.m. 10.0 a.m. 10.0 a.m. 8.20 p.m.	**Day Trip to ILFRACOMBE** Leave Ilfracombe 6.35 p.m. for Porthcawl. **Day Trip to ILFRACOMBE and Cruise to off CLOVELLY.** Fare to include Cruise 15s.6d. Passengers for Cruise change Steamers at Ilfracombe in each direction. Steamer leaves Ilfracombe for Cruise at 3.0 p.m. **Single Trip to MINEHEAD, LYNMOUTH and ILFRACOMBE.** **Single Trip to BARRY, WESTON, CLEVEDON and BRISTOL.** Note.—Steamer leaves Swansea 9.0 a.m. for Porthcawl.
WEDNESDAY, JULY 7th.	10.15 a.m. 9.40 p.m.	**Day Trip to ILFRACOMBE and LUNDY ISLAND (to land)** Leave Lundy Island 4.30 p.m. Ilfracombe 6.15 p.m. (via Swansea) for Porthcawl. **Single Trip to SWANSEA.** Note.—Steamer leaves Swansea 9.15 a.m. for Porthcawl. Steamer leaves Swansea 8.30 p.m. for Porthcawl.
SUNDAY, JULY 11th.	2.30 p.m. 4.45 p.m.	**Afternoon Cruise passing ST. DONATS** Back about 4.35 p.m. Fare 4s. **Single Trip to ILFRACOMBE.** Note.—Steamer leaves Ilfracombe 11.45 a.m. for Porthcawl.
SUNDAY, JULY 18th.	10.15 a.m. 9.0 p.m.	**Day Trip to ILFRACOMBE** Leave Ilfracombe 5.30 p.m. (via Swansea) for Porthcawl. **Single Trip to SWANSEA.** Note.—Steamer leaves Swansea 9.15 a.m. for Porthcawl.
MONDAY, JULY 19th.	10.30 a.m. 7.30 p.m.	**Day Trip to ILFRACOMBE** Leave Ilfracombe 5.45 p.m. for Porthcawl. **Single Trip to BARRY, WESTON, CLEVEDON and BRISTOL.** Note.—Steamer leaves Swansea 9.30 a.m. for Porthcawl.
SUNDAY, JULY 25th.	2.15 p.m. 4.15 p.m.	**Afternoon Cruise towards ST. DONATS** Back about 4.0 p.m. Fare 4s. **Single Trip to ILFRACOMBE.** Note.—Steamer leaves Ilfracombe 11.45 a.m. for Porthcawl.

FARES FROM PORTHCAWL

	Single	Day Return		Single	Day Return
ILFRACOMBE	12s. 6d.	12s. 6d.	SWANSEA	5s. 0d.	—
LUNDY ISLAND	18s. 6d.	18s. 6d.	PORT TALBOT	4s. 0d.	—
WESTON	12s. 6d.	12s. 6d.	BARRY	9s. 0d.	—
MINEHEAD	10s. 0d.	—	CLEVEDON or BRISTOL	12s. 6d.	—

P.T.O.

A 1954 timetable with details of the Centenary Year.

The *Bristol Queen* on the first post-war visit to Clovelly, on Wednesday 16 June 1954.

The *Cardiff Queen* arriving at Bideford on Wednesday 14 July 1954. This was the first call by a White Funnel steamer at the North Devon town for thirty years.

The photographer's daughters watch the *Britannia* steaming down the River Avon on Sunday 27 June 1954.

The *Ravenswood* leaving Cardiff in 1954. During that year the four pre-war steamers were fitted with full mainmasts in order to carry the navigation lights necessary to comply with the new regulations for the prevention of collision at sea.

The *Britannia* at Minehead on Wednesday 28 July 1954.

The *Bristol Queen* on the first post-war trip to Tenby on Thursday 12 August 1954.

The engine
room of the
Glen Usk.

The *Glen Usk* at
Swansea on
Saturday
4 September
1954.

The *Glen Usk* leaving Weston in 1954.

The *Glen Usk* in the River Avon, 1954.

The *Britannia* and *Ravenswood* in the Merchant's Dock, Bristol, in March 1955. Despite the company's efforts to improve its situation in the 1954 season, the appalling weather led to a poor financial result. The *Ravenswood* failed her five-yearly Board of Trade survey and was offered for sale. The *Empress Queen*, laid up since 1952, was sold to Greek buyers in March 1955. The other steamers, however, were prepared for the forthcoming season.

The only dry dock in Bristol was at Charles Hill's Yard, but was not wide enough to accommodate the two *Queens*. They, therefore, had to be dry docked in Avonmouth. The *Cardiff Queen* is seen making the short journey down river for that purpose in March 1955.

The *Bristol Queen* in dry dock at Avonmouth in 1955.

Painting in progress on the *Glen Usk* in Hill's dry dock, Bristol, in 1955.

The *Britannia* had suffered serious paddle trouble at the end of the stormy 1954 season. She is seen here undergoing repairs at the Underfall Yard, early in 1955.

Tuesday 31 May 1955. With her repairs and repainting well under way, the *Britannia* is almost ready for another season.

P. & A. CAMPBELL LIMITED
Passenger Steamship Owners

25 OLD STEINE
BRIGHTON, 1
Telephone: BRIGHTON 28714

1955

"NO-PASSPORT" DAY EXCURSIONS

Dear Sir/Madam,

We have pleasure in giving preliminary details of the "No-Passport" Cross-Channel sailings from Newhaven and Eastbourne to Boulogne.

Coaches have been arranged between Hastings and Eastbourne and special trains between Brighton and Eastbourne. Return fares from Brighton, Newhaven, Eastbourne or Hastings will be **38/6d.**, including coach or rail fare where applicable.

As a special inducement to parents to travel with their children, a reduced fare of only **22/6d.** will be charged for children up to 16 years of age.

All that will be required by passengers will be two passport-sized photographs. Passengers who already have passports will be able to use these, without need for photographs. Neither photograph nor passport will be needed by children.

A restaurant with full catering facilities and fully licensed bars will be available on board the Steamer.

From Boulogne, a Coach Tour will be run to Le Touquet-Paris Plage, the fare being **11/6d.** for adults and **7/-** for children under twelve years of age.

If sailings are cancelled for any reason (and the Company reserve the right to effect such cancellations) the sums paid in fares will be returned in full.

A brochure giving complete details is being published and a copy will shortly be sent to you.

Meanwhile we suggest that you book individually or for parties, in respect of which special reduced rates apply. Thus intending passengers can insure reservations for these excursions.

In addition to the Cross-Channel Service, sailings from Brighton, Eastbourne and Hastings to the Isle of Wight and elsewhere will be run as in previous years.

Yours faithfully,
P. & A. CAMPBELL LTD.
J. B. MACDOUGALL
South Coast Manager.

SEE REVERSE SIDE FOR TIME TABLE

The company's negotiations with the Government regarding 'No Passport' trips to France were satisfactorily concluded in time for the 1955 season. A letter was issued to intending passengers including the *Glen Gower's* cross-Channel timetable (opposite page).

54

TIME TABLE OF SAILINGS

	Depart Newhaven	Depart Eastbourne	Arrive Boulogne	Depart Boulogne	Arrive Eastbourne	Arrive Newhaven
JUNE						
Thur. 23rd ...	9.15 a.m.	11.00 a.m.	2.40 p.m.	7.00 p.m.	10.45 p.m.	11.50 p.m.
Fri. 24th ...	9.30 a.m.	11.40 a.m.	3.20 p.m.	7.50 p.m.	11.30 p.m.	12.30 a.m.
Tues. 28th ...	9.00 a.m.	10.30 a.m.	2.10 p.m.	6.00 p.m.	9.45 p.m.	10.50 p.m.
Thur. 30th ...	9.00 a.m.	10.30 a.m.	2.10 p.m.	6.00 p.m.	9.45 p.m.	10.50 p.m.
JULY						
Tues. 5th ...	9.00 a.m.	10.30 a.m.	2.10 p.m.	6.00 p.m.	9.45 p.m.	10.50 p.m.
Thur. 7th ...	9.00 a.m.	10.30 a.m.	2.10 p.m.	6.00 p.m.	9.45 p.m.	10.50 p.m.
Wed. 13th ...	9.00 a.m.	10.30 a.m.	2.10 p.m.	6.00 p.m.	9.45 p.m.	10.50 p.m.
Thur. 14th ...	9.00 a.m.	10.30 a.m.	2.10 p.m.	6.00 p.m.	9.45 p.m.	10.50 p.m.
Sun. 17th ...	9.00 a.m.	10.30 a.m.	2.10 p.m.	6.00 p.m.	9.45 p.m.	10.50 p.m.
Wed. 20th ...	9.00 a.m.	10.30 a.m.	2.10 p.m.	6.00 p.m.	9.45 p.m.	10.50 p.m.
Thur. 21st ...	9.00 a.m.	10.30 a.m.	2.10 p.m.	6.00 p.m.	9.45 p.m.	10.50 p.m.
Wed. 27th ...	9.00 a.m.	10.30 a.m.	2.10 p.m.	6.00 p.m.	9.45 p.m.	10.50 p.m.
Thur. 28th ...	9.00 a.m.	10.30 a.m.	2.10 p.m.	6.00 p.m.	9.45 p.m.	10.50 p.m.
Sun. 31st ...	9.00 a.m.	10.30 a.m.	2.10 p.m.	5.30 p.m.	9.15 p.m.	—
AUGUST						
Tues. 2nd ...	9.00 a.m.	10.30 a.m.	2.10 p.m.	6.00 p.m.	9.45 p.m.	10.50 p.m.
Wed. 3rd ...	9.00 a.m.	10.30 a.m.	2.10 p.m.	6.00 p.m.	9.45 p.m.	10.50 p.m.
Sun. 7th ...	9.30 a.m.	11.00 a.m.	2.45 p.m.	7.00 p.m.	10.40 p.m.	11.45 p.m.
Thur. 11th ...	—	9.30 a.m.	1.15 p.m.	5.30 p.m.	9.15 p.m.	10.30 p.m.
Sat. 13th ...	9.00 a.m.	10.30 a.m.	2.10 p.m.	6.00 p.m.	9.45 p.m.	10.50 p.m.
Tues. 16th ...	9.00 a.m.	10.30 a.m.	2.10 p.m.	6.00 p.m.	9.45 p.m.	10.50 p.m.
Wed. 17th ...	9.00 a.m.	10.30 a.m.	2.10 p.m.	6.00 p.m.	9.45 p.m.	10.50 p.m.
Thur. 18th ...	9.00 a.m.	10.30 a.m.	2.10 p.m.	6.00 p.m.	9.45 p.m.	10.50 p.m.
Sun. 21st ...	9.30 a.m.	11.00 a.m.	2.40 p.m.	7.00 p.m.	10.45 p.m.	11.50 p.m.
Thur. 25th ...	9.00 a.m.	10.30 a.m.	2.10 p.m.	6.00 p.m.	9.45 p.m.	10.50 p.m.
Fri. 26th ...	9.00 a.m.	10.30 a.m.	2.10 p.m.	6.00 p.m.	9.45 p.m.	10.50 p.m.
Sun. 28th ...	9.00 a.m.	10.30 a.m.	2.10 p.m.	5.30 p.m.	9.15 p.m.	10.40 p.m.
Wed. 31st ...	9.00 a.m.	10.30 a.m.	2.10 p.m.	6.00 p.m.	9.45 p.m.	10.50 p.m.
SEPTEMBER						
Thur. 1st ...	9.00 a.m.	10.30 a.m.	2.10 p.m.	6.00 p.m.	9.45 p.m.	10.50 p.m.
Mon. 5th ...	—	10.30 a.m.	2.10 p.m.	6.30 p.m.	10.20 p.m.	11.30 p.m.
Fri. 9th ...	7.30 a.m.	9.00 a.m.	12.40 p.m.	4.40 p.m.	8.20 p.m.	9.20 p.m.
Tues. 13th ...	9.00 a.m.	10.30 a.m.	2.10 p.m.	6.00 p.m.	9.45 p.m.	10.50 p.m.
Thur. 15th ...	9.00 a.m.	10.30 a.m.	2.10 p.m.	5.00 p.m.	8.45 p.m.	9.50 p.m.
Sun. 18th ...	9.00 a.m.	10.30 a.m.	2.10 p.m.	6.00 p.m.	9.45 p.m.	10.50 p.m.

Subject to the Company's Conditions of Carriage

The 'Passport Essential' trips to France in 1954 had not been a success. There were only eight such crossings scheduled, four of which were cancelled because of bad weather. In 1955, however, there were no cancellations and some 16,000 passengers made the journey to Boulogne. The *Glen Gower* entered service in the Bristol Channel for a short time and is seen, above, rounding the River Avon's notorious Horseshoe Bend.

The *Glen Gower* leaving Boulogne later in the 1955 season.

The *Britannia* leaving Newport on a cruise to Bristol, 1955.

The *Cardiff Queen* leaving Bideford on Saturday 2 July 1955.

The *Cardiff Queen* at Tenby on Sunday 17 July 1955.

The *Britannia* at the Pier Head, Cardiff in 1955.

The *Cardiff Queen* at Milford Haven on Monday 8 August 1955. A trip run in conjunction with a visit of Her Majesty the Queen in the Royal Yacht *Britannia* to West Wales.

The *Bristol Queen*, outward bound in the River Avon in 1955.

Sunday 2 October 1955. The *Glen Gower* at Ilfracombe on the homeward trip from Brighton to Bristol.

The *Glen Gower* and *Glen Usk* at Ilfracombe on Sunday 2 October 1955.

The *Ravenswood* was sold to the Newport Ship-breakers, John Cashmore & Son, in the autumn of 1955. She is seen here being towed down the River Avon to their berth on the River Usk, on Thursday 20 October.

The *Ravenswood* at Cashmore's Yard, October 1955. She had been the first vessel built specifically for Campbells Bristol Channel trade in 1891 and was the longest serving White Funnel steamer with sixty-four years of continual service for her company and her country behind her!

SUNSHINE AND

ISTOL FASHION!

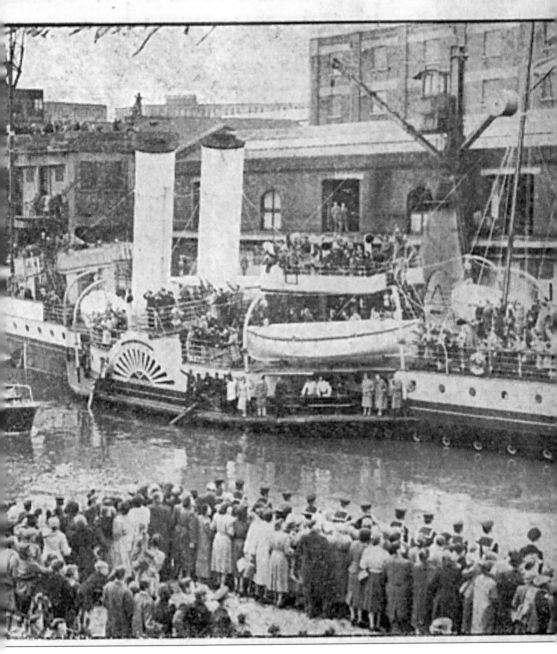

The *Glen Usk* arriving at Barry, Sunday 27 May 1956.

The *Britannia* arriving at Hotwells Landing Stage, Bristol, in 1956.

Previous page: A Royal visit to Bristol with the *Glen Gower* in attendance.

On the afternoon of Sunday 19 August 1956, the *Bristol Queen*, half an hour after leaving Ilfracombe for Tenby, developed paddle trouble which rendered her immobile. A radio message for assistance was sent to the *Cardiff Queen*, which had just left Ilfracombe for Mumbles and Swansea. The *Cardiff Queen* reached her sister ship about an hour later and is seen, above, manoeuvring in order to reach her with a tow rope.

The *Cardiff Queen* towed the *Bristol Queen* across the channel to Swansea. She is seen above in the River Avon on the following evening after having been towed from Swansea to Bristol for repairs.

A further summer of bad weather and the consequent loss of business led to the withdrawal of the *Britannia* after sixty years of service. She is seen here leaving Bristol on her 'Farewell Cruise' to Ilfracombe on Wednesday 19 September 1956.

The *Britannia* leaving Ilfracombe Pier to anchor offshore before her return to Bristol. Ironically, this was not to be her final trip. She ran for a further week when she was required to replace the *Glen Usk* on the Cardiff-to-Weston ferry.

The *Britannia* leaving Penarth for the breakers yard. Friday 7 December 1956.

The *Britannia* at Cashmores Yard, Newport. December 1956.

The *Glen Gower* leaving Ilfracombe for the last time, on Sunday 29 September 1957. The company ceased its paddle steamer operations on the South Coast at the end of the 1956 season. During 1957 the *Glen Gower* had replaced the *Glen Usk* on the Cardiff-Weston ferry, the latter being out of service for the whole season owing to boiler trouble. Similar afflictions dogged the *Glen Gower* herself and brought about her withdrawal from service at the end of the year.

In order to maintain a link with the South Coast, the company chartered the motor vessel *Crested Eagle* from the General Steam Navigation Co., for the 1957 season. She is seen here arriving at Brighton. The appalling weather and persistent mechanical problems rendered the charter a dismal failure and brought a sad end to the company's South Coast services.

At the end of the 1958 season, P&A Campbell Ltd went into receivership. The receiver, however, was most reluctant for the company to cease operations and suggested that two ships should be put into service for the summer of 1959 in the hope that, with more favourable weather, a better financial result would be obtained. The receiver's judgement was proved to be correct; a fine summer generated a small but, nevertheless, most welcome profit. The two ships in service were the *Glen Usk*, above, and the *Cardiff Queen*, left. The *Bristol Queen* was laid up in Penarth Dock.

On the evening of Saturday 30 August 1959, the *Glen Usk* left Bristol an hour later than scheduled. While rounding the Horseshoe Bend, the rapid flow of the falling tide forced her on to the mud of the Gloucestershire bank and held her fast. Her passengers were quickly disembarked and returned home by alternative transport.

The *Glen Usk* heeled over to an alarming angle during the night as the tide receded, but refloated during the early hours of the following morning. She was towed to Penarth Dock where an inspection showed her to be little the worse for her experience. She returned to service a few days later.

Three
The 1960s

The *Bristol Queen* at Porthcawl, Sunday 25 June 1961.

Above and below: Since her withdrawal from service at the end of 1957, the *Glen Gower* had been laid up in Penarth Dock. She was offered for sale and was eventually purchased by Belgian ship-breakers. She is seen leaving Penarth for Antwerp in tow of the Hull tug *Tradesman*, in April 1960.

The *Glen Usk* on Penarth pontoon, in preparation for the 1960 season.

A Royal visit to Cardiff. The *Glen Usk* escorting the Royal Yacht *Britannia* off Penarth Head on Saturday 6 August 1960.

The *Cardiff Queen*, *Bristol Queen* and *Glen Usk* in Penarth Dock, Sunday 12 March 1961. The season of 1960 had been the last one for the *Glen Usk*. Escalating coal costs forced the company to withdraw her and bring the oil-burning *Bristol Queen* back into service for 1961.

The *Bristol Queen* on Penarth pontoon, March 1961.

The *Bristol Queen* arriving at Porthcawl on Sunday 25 June 1961.

Friday 30 June 1961. The *Bristol Queen* arriving at the dock entrance, Newport, on the annual charter to the Newport Harbour Commissioners.

The *Cardiff Queen* arriving at Barry on Tuesday 24 April 1962.

The *Bristol Queen* arriving at Tenby on Sunday 15 July 1962.

During the winter of 1962-1963 the *Bristol Queen* underwent an extensive engine overhaul at the yard of Cosens & Co., the South Coast pleasure steamer operators. She is seen, above, arriving in Weymouth harbour on Wednesday 14 November 1962.

With her overhaul complete, the *Bristol Queen* awaits her return to the Bristol Channel in March 1963.

In 1963 the motor vessel *St Trillo* joined the Campbell fleet from the North Wales Steamship Co. She was to maintain the ferry service during the early and late periods of the seasons when the limited number of passengers made the running of the *Queens* unprofitable. The *St Trillo* is seen here on her arrival at Cardiff on 13 March 1963.

Thursday 11 April 1963. The *St Trillo*, now painted in Campbells' colours, at the Pier Head, Cardiff, about to leave on the first trip of the season, to Weston. The *Cardiff Queen* lies alongside and have just completed compass adjusting.

Above and below: The arrival of the *St Trillo* made the future of the *Glen Usk* very uncertain; in fact, within a matter of weeks the latter was sold for scrap. The *Glen Usk* is seen leaving Cardiff for breaking up at Passage West, Cork, on Monday 29 April 1963.

The *Bristol Queen* at Penzance on Saturday 18 May 1963. Three-day trips to the Isles of Scilly had been an occasional feature of the pre-1914 timetables. The last such sailing is believed to have been that of the *Britannia* in 1907, when the return fare was £1 0s 0d!

The *Bristol Queen* at St Mary's, Isles of Scilly, 18 May 1963.

Opposite: The timetable for the *Bristol Queen*'s Isles or Scilly excursion.

White Funnel Fleet

Special Week-end Excursion

By the BRISTOL QUEEN

to

PENZANCE

and

ISLES OF SCILLY

FRIDAY, MAY 17th

Leave Cardiff 9.45 a.m., Weston 10.45 a.m., Ilfracombe 2.0 p.m.
Due Penzance 9.45 p.m.

SATURDAY, MAY 18th

Leave Penzance 10.45 a.m., due Scilly Isles 1.45 p.m.
Leave Scilly Isles 6.15 p.m., due Penzance 9.0 p.m.

SUNDAY, MAY 19th

Leave Penzance 9.30 a.m., due Ilfracombe 5.0 p.m., Barry 8.10 p.m.,
Clevedon 9.45 p.m.

Fares :

From CARDIFF or WESTON and return to Barry or Clevedon :
  To Penzance £7 10s.; To Isles of Scilly £9.
  Single fare to Penzance £5 10s.; To Isles of Scilly £7.
From ILFRACOMBE :
  To Penzance (Single) £4 10s.. (Return) £6.
  To Isles of Scilly (Single) £6; (Return) £7 10s.

For the convenience and comfort of passengers the numbers carried between Ilfracombe and Penzance, and Penzance and the Isles of Scilly will be limited to 250

General Information :—

CATERING. Meals and light refreshments will be obtainable at moderate prices on board the steamer. The vessel is fully licensed.

ACCOMMODATION. Passengers make their own arrangements for accommodation at Penzance, and the company will be pleased to assist in this regard if desired.

COUPONS and SEASON TICKETS are not available for this excursion.

CONDITIONS OF CARRIAGE. All tickets are issued and passengers carried subject to the Company's conditions of carriage as exhibited on Piers, at the Company's Offices, Agencies, and on their steamers.

Sailings are subject to weather and circumstances. In the event of a cancellation for any reason whatsoever of any of the above sailings, fares will be refunded in respect of the portion of the journey not carried out, and no further liability shall be accepted by the Company.

For further particulars apply to :

P. & A. CAMPBELL LTD., Pier Gates (Birnbeck Pier), Weston-super-Mare ; Tel. 6784. 10 The Quay, Ilfracombe; Tel. 687. 3 Britannia Buildings Cumberland Basin, Bristol; Tel. 23112; any other offices of the Company ; or to Head Office, 4 Dock Chambers, Cardiff. Tel. 20255

T. & W. Goulding Ltd.

Left and below: Aboard the *Bristol Queen*, Wednesday 26 June 1963.

The *Cardiff Queen*, outward bound from Cardiff on Sunday 7 July 1963.

The *Cardiff Queen* awaits her passengers for the final sailing of the day from Weston to Penarth and Cardiff on Sunday 21 July 1963.

AMENDED SAILINGS

SEASON 1964

The WHITE FUNNEL FLEET

BRISTOL QUEEN   CARDIFF QUEEN
GLEN GOWER   GLEN USK

SAILINGS FROM

● CHEPSTOW

(BUFFER WHARF)

by the M.V. St. Trillo

SUNDAY, SEPTEMBER 20th, 1964

GRAND DAY TRIP TO CLEVEDON, WESTON AND BARRY

Leave Chepstow 8.15 a.m., due to arrive Clevedon 9.45 a.m., Weston 10.35 a.m., Barry 11.40 a.m. Leave Barry 2.30 p.m., Weston 3.40 p.m., Clevedon 4.30 p.m., due Chepstow 6.30 p.m.

Fares (Single or Day Return) :

Clevedon 10/-, Weston or Barry 15/- (Children half-price)

● SINGLE TRIP TO PORTISHEAD, CLEVEDON, WESTON AND BARRY

Leave Chepstow 7.0 p.m.

Fares : Portishead or Clevedon 10/-, Weston or Barry 15/-

Note : The St. Trillo leaves Portishead 5.20 p.m. for Chepstow

---

● *For further particulars and conditions of carriage please see overleaf*

Another revival of the 1960s was the occasional trip to Chepstow. The Monmouthshire town had been a frequent port of call for the White Funnel steamers in the years before the Great War, but the visits ceased after 1914. The *St Trillo* revived the sailings fifty years later.

The *St Trillo* at Chepstow, turning to berth at Buffer Wharf. In the background is one of the ferries which took passengers and cars across the River Severn, from Beachley to Aust, before the opening of the Severn Bridge in August 1966.

Above and below: On Wednesday 16 September 1964 a severe gale swept through the Bristol Channel. The *Bristol Queen* was stormbound at Swansea and the *Cardiff Queen* experienced several rough crossings between Cardiff and Weston. The photographs on this page were taken on her afternoon trip.

Above and below: With great difficulty the *Cardiff Queen* berthed at Weston Pier and the few passengers aboard were disembarked quickly across a wildly lurching gangway. She left to return to Cardiff and all of her sailings for the rest of the day were cancelled.

Easter Sunday 18 April 1965. The two *Queens* present a rather unusual picture mottled with anti-rust paint, in the Queen Alexandra Dock, in Cardiff.

The *Bristol Queen* leaving Clevedon Pier on Wednesday 5 May 1965.

The *Bristol Queen* leaving Cardiff on Sunday 9 May 1965.

The *Bristol Queen* in the River Avon on Tuesday 11 May 1965.

Sunday 16 May 1965. The *Bristol Queen* leaving Ilfracombe for a cruise on the first visit of the season.

The *Cardiff Queen* arriving at Mumbles Pier on Thursday 27 May 1965.

Whit-Sunday 6 June 1965. The *Bristol Queen* arriving at Penarth.

The *Cardiff Queen* at Cardiff. Thursday 10 June 1965.

The *Bristol Queen* developed paddle trouble as she arrived at Penarth from Ilfracombe on Sunday 20 June 1965. She is seen here at anchor off Penarth while temporary repairs were effected. The *Cardiff Queen* approaches the pier, bound for Weston.

While berthing at Weston in early August 1965, the *Cardiff Queen*'s full complement of passengers waiting to disembark, caused her to list heavily to starboard. The tide forced her against the jetty and crumpled the bridge wing. It was temporarily repaired with plywood, as seen in this view of her at Cardiff on Thursday 5 August 1965.

The *Cardiff Queen* re-embarking her passengers off Clovelly on Thursday 5 August 1965.

The *Bristol Queen* at Padstow on Sunday 8 August 1965. The first visit of a White Funnel steamer to the Cornish port since the *Devonia* in August 1938.

Opposite: The timetable for the *Bristol Queen*' trip to Padstow.

COME   ABOARD!

YOUR FIRST OPPORTUNITY SINCE 1938 TO SAIL TO

PADSTOW

PADDLE STEAMER

"BRISTOL QUEEN"

SAILS FROM ILFRACOMBE
(WITH CONNECTIONS FROM CARDIFF & SWANSEA)

on

SUNDAY, 8th AUGUST, 1965

Leave ILFRACOMBE 10.45 a.m.   Leave PADSTOW   3.45 p.m.
Arrive PADSTOW   2.45 p.m.   Arrive ILFRACOMBE 7.35 p.m.

SINGLE OR RETURN FARE FROM ILFRACOMBE 26/6

NOTE—Tickets may be purchased prior to sailing day at a

SPECIAL CHEAP RATE of **22/6** (Children half fares)

Weekly and Season Tickets not valid for this excursion, but
holders of such tickets can purchase their steamer tickets
at half rates. Coupons and free passes not valid.

FULL CATERING FACILITIES
LICENSED BARS OPEN THROUGHOUT THE VOYAGE
AMPLE LOUNGES & COVERED ACCOMMODATION
ON BOARD

COME ALONG AND ENJOY THIS MAGNIFICENT CRUISE ON ONE OF
BRITAIN'S FASTEST AND MOST MODERN PADDLE STEAMERS ALONG
THE GLORIOUS NORTH DEVON & CORNISH COASTS, PASSING BULL
POINT, HARTLAND POINT, BUDE, TINTAGEL, Etc.

For full details of connections and through fares from CARDIFF, SWANSEA and
MUMBLES see Messrs. P. & A. CAMPBELL'S Sailing Bills.

*Promoted by The Paddle Steamer Preservation Society, with the co-operation
of P. & A. Campbell Ltd., under whose Conditions of Carriage, as
exhibited at their Offices and on board their ships all passengers are
carried. Sailing subject to weather and circumstances, but should
the excursion be cancelled fares paid in advance will be
refunded.*

TICKETS OBTAINABLE ON BOARD OR IN ADVANCE FROM :
P. & A. Campbell Ltd., 10 The Quay, Ilfracombe, Devon.
or by post from
Mr. P. J. Murrell, 23 Barley Croft, Westbury-on-Trym, Bristol.

T. & W. Goulding Ltd.

Left and below: Seen from the *Bristol Queen*, the *Cardiff Queen* arrives at Ilfracombe Pier on Wednesday 9 September 1965. The *Bristol Queen*'s scheduled trip to Bideford had been cancelled owing to bad weather. The *Cardiff Queen* had attempted to reach Lundy but heavy seas forced her to return before reaching her destination.

Towards the end of the 1965 season the company purchased the motor vessel *Vecta* from the Red Funnel Line of Southampton. She is seen at the Pier Head, Cardiff, on Wednesday 22 September 1965.

The *Vecta* leaving Weston on Wednesday 6 October 1965.

During the winter months a variety of alterations were carried out to the *Vecta*, including the conversion of her car-carrying space, on the main deck, amidships, into a saloon. She is seen arriving at Cardiff on Saturday 9 April 1966, having been renamed, *Westward Ho*.

The vagaries of the British weather. The *Westward Ho* at the Pier Head, Cardiff on Thursday 14 April 1966. All sailings have been cancelled owing to heavy snow!

The *Westward Ho* leaving Cardiff on Sunday 17 April 1966.

The *Westward Ho* in the River Avon on Sunday 1 May 1966.

During the mid-1960s the Swedish-Amerika Line scheduled visits to the Bristol Channel as part of its 'Springtime Cruises'. The ships anchored in Walton Bay and the White Funnel steamers took their passengers to and from Avonmouth. In the above view the *Bristol Queen* approaches the *Kungsholm* on 5 May 1965 and below, the *Westward Ho* approaches the *Gripsholm* on 4 May 1966.

Above and below: The *Westward Ho* at Avonmouth on Wednesday 4 May 1966.

Saturday 18 June 1966. The *Westward Ho* on her first visit to Watchet.

The *Westward Ho* arrives at Minehead on her first call on Saturday 18 June 1966.

The *Westward Ho* proved herself to be a very capable ship. Despite the fact that she had been built for operation in the sheltered waters of the Solent, she coped well with the strong tides and rough seas of the Bristol Channel. These qualities were put to the test on the evening of 22 May 1966 when she encountered very heavy weather in the channel. She is seen above approaching Weston Pier on that occasion.

The *Westward Ho* alongside the *Cardiff Queen* at Penarth Pier on Sunday 26 June 1966. The *Cardiff Queen* had been instructed to delay her departure from the pier to embark a 'party' who had missed her at Cardiff and who were to be trans-shipped from the *Westward Ho*. The motor vessel duly tied up alongside the *Cardiff Queen* and the 'party' – consisting of one person – embarked in grand style amid the cheers and applause of the passengers!

BRISTOL QUEEN RAM
PIER AT PENARTH

THE P. and A. Campbell steamer Bristol Queen rammed Penarth Pier today in heavy mist, but the 120 people aboard and 50 others waiting on the pier to board the ship escaped injury.

The 600-ton vessel was jammed in the collision and there were fears she would be swept further under the pier by the outgoing tide.

The pier was cleared as a precautionary measure.

The Bristol Queen was edging towards the pier when, it was believed, the tide and wind caught her.

An eye-witness said: "There was a loud crash and the steamer banged into the pier. One of the pier stays jammed into her paddle and she was caught.

It happened at high tide after fog warnings went out.

Two tugs are
called in

A passenger said: "They seemed to shut off the engines just before she berthed and then the wind and tide appeared to take her into the pier."

The steamer had sailed from Cardiff and was due to pick up passengers at Penarth before going on to Ilfracombe.

It was understood that the company were sending a relief steamer, the Westward Ho, to collect the Bristol Queen passengers.

Two tugs were called from Cardiff to pull the Bristol Queen away fro mthe pier.

First reports said the collision severed a water pipe and power lines.

Pier authorities said they had been unable to assess the damage to the pier structure.

Eye-witnesses said the tide swept the Bristol Queen four times against the pier, damaging the structure severely. Visibility was reported as down to 15 yards.

● The Bristol Queen, pictured alongside Penarth Pier today after colliding with the pier in heavy sea mist. In the foreground can be seen damage to the pier.

A newspaper report of a mishap to the *Bristol Queen* in thick fog on the morning of Friday 19 August 1966. The report was much exaggerated: the steamer did not 'ram' the pier but approached it about halfway out from the landward end. She slowed down but the strong ebb tide forced her broadside on. Two tugs were called in order to tow her clear but, in doing so, they pulled her along the pier instead of away from it, causing some structural damage. The *Bristol Queen*, however, resumed service on the following day.

Sunday 18 September 1966. 'Down below' on the *Cardiff Queen*. Above, outside the engine room and, below, the dining saloon.

The successful operation of the *Westward Ho* and the soaring costs of running and maintaining the two *Queens*, made the future of the latter very uncertain. In 1967 the *Cardiff Queen* was laid up and placed on the market. She is shown in the Graving Dock at Barry.

Aboard the *Bristol Queen* leaving Swansea on Sunday 2 July 1967. On Saturday 26 August she struck a submerged obstruction off Barry which caused major paddle damage, and she was withdrawn from service.

The *Bristol Queen* laid up in the Queen Alexandra Dock, Cardiff, in August 1967. In order to maintain the company's advertised services, the *Westward Ho* was joined by the *St Trillo* in the Bristol Channel. She was, in turn, replaced in North Wales by the motor vessel *Queen of the Isles*, on charter from the Isles of Scilly Steamship Co.

In January 1968 the *Bristol Queen* was struck by the Liberian tanker *Geodor*, manoeuvring in the dock in high winds The *Bristol Queen*'s foremast and jackstaff were broken and she sustained extensive damage to her starboard bow rail and bridge wing.

Above and below: The *Cardiff Queen* was sold early in 1968 for use as a floating nightclub on the River Usk. She was towed into position on the morning of Wednesday 29 February but as the tide fell she broke away from her moorings and slid broadside on to the river. She refloated later in the day and was towed into Newport Dock. Once again she was advertised for sale.

Above and below: The *Bristol Queen* had also been placed on the market and was sold to Belgian ship-breakers. She left Cardiff in tow of the German tug *Fairplay X1* on the afternoon of Wednesday 21 March 1968 and was handed over to the breakers at Flushing five days later.

Above and below: The *Cardiff Queen* was sold to the Newport ship-breakers, John Cashmore, and left Newport Dock for their yard on the River Usk on the afternoon of Tuesday 9 April 1968.

The *Cardiff Queen* at Cashmore's Yard on Thursday 11 April 1968.

Within a matter of weeks the *Cardiff Queen* was reduced to a pile of scrap metal on the quayside. This final photograph of the last White Funnel paddle steamer was taken in mid-April, when her demolition was already well advanced.

The Bristol Channel services were maintained in 1968 by the *St Trillo* and the *Westward Ho*. The company once again chartered the *Queen of the Isles* to run on the North Wales coast, but she visited the Bristol Channel in order to carry out the annual Isles of Scilly excursion. She is seen here at the Pier Head, Cardiff, after her arrival from Penzance on Thursday 23 May 1968.

At the end of the 1968 season the *Queen of the Isles* again returned to Cardiff to run a trip around the coast to Ilfracombe, Penzance, Weymouth, Bournemouth, Eastbourne, Hastings, Dover and London. This was by way of an experiment, the company considering running her on the Sussex coast and the River Thames during the following season. She is seen arriving at Ilfracombe, with the *Westward Ho*, on her journey south on 14 September 1968.

In May 1969 a further vessel was added to the Campbell fleet: the Red Funnel Line's motor vessel *Balmoral*, seen at Cardiff shortly after her arrival from the South Coast. The decade drew to a close on an optimistic note; the *Balmoral* and *Westward Ho* maintained the Bristol Channel services, the *St Trillo* ran on the North Wales coast, and the *Queen of the Isles* spent a reasonably successful, but not particularly lucrative season on the Sussex coast and on the Thames. The coastal passenger trade in general was, however, subject to many 'peaks and troughs'. It would have been a brave person who would venture to predict the patterns of events of the 1970s!

Four
The 1970s and Beyond

At the end of the 1969 season P&A Campbell Ltd terminated its charter of the *Queen of the Isles* and the ship was returned to her owners. During the course of the following few years the *St Trillo* and *Westward Ho* were disposed of and the *Balmoral* maintained the Bristol Channel services alone until the end of 1981, when she was sold for conversion to a floating restaurant in Dundee. The tradition which the Campbell brothers had started in the 1880s appeared to have ended. However, that was not the case. The Clyde paddle steamer, *Waverley*, the last sea-going paddle steamer in the world, had been purchased, in 1974, by a company formed by members of the Paddle Steamer Preservation Society. Her tentative beginnings in Scotland in the mid-1970s rapidly grew and developed into regular 'Round Britain' journeys, the first of her annual visits to the Bristol Channel taking place in 1979. She is seen, above, leaving Penarth Pier on Monday 15 June 1981.

Previous page: The *Waverley* arriving at Minehead Harbour on Sunday 14 June 1981.

Above and below: The *Waverley* at Minehead on Sunday 14 June 1981.

Saturday 13 June 1981. The *Waverley* passing beneath the Severn Bridge.

Above and below: The *Waverley* at Newport on Friday 19 June 1981.

The *Waverley* leaving Mumbles on Friday 4 June 1981.

The *Waverley* at Porthcawl on Friday 4 June 1981.

The *Waverley* leaving Sharpness on Friday 11 June 1981.

The *Waverley* at Avonmouth on Friday 11 June 1981.

Weston-super-Mare's Birnbeck Pier had fallen into a state of disrepair and could no longer be used by the steamers. The *Waverley*, however, revived the sailings to the Somerset resort on Monday 21 June 1981. She is seen, above, passing the derelict Birnbeck Pier and, below, at anchor off the Grand Pier in Weston Bay, landing her passengers in motor boats. Berthing is now accomplished at the Knightstone jetty.

In May 1981 the *Waverley*'s operations were augmented by the motor vessel, *Prince Ivanhoe*, the former Portsmouth-to-Isle of Wight ferry, *Shanklin*. She began running in the Bristol Channel in May and is seen here leaving Penarth in June 1981. The vessel's untimely and most unfortunate end occured two months later when, off the Gower coast, her hull was holed by an underwater obstruction. She was immediately beached at Port Eynon, where all her passengers and crew were safety taken ashore but the *Prince Ivanhoe* became a constructive total loss.

On Sunday 17 April 1983 the *Waverley* was on charter to the North Devon Hospital Board. She is seen at Bideford shortly before her departure on a day trip to Lundy Island.

The *Waverley* off Lundy on Sunday 17 April 1983.

In October 1986, on her return to Scotland from the South Coast and the River Thames, the *Waverley* paid a further visit to the Bristol Channel. She made her first call at Bristol on that occasion and is seen here in the City Docks on Friday 3 October 1986.

The *Waverley* steaming down the River Avon on Sunday 5 October 1986. She was the first paddle steamer to do so since the *Bristol Queen* in 1967.

Following the loss of the *Prince Ivanhoe*, a new consort for the *Waverley* was sought. Eventually the *Balmoral*, lying in Dundee in deplorable condition, was purchased in 1986. After considerable re-plating of her hull and interior renovation, she began a hectic schedule. Prior to and after high summer in the Bristol Channel, she has visited a wide variety of ports and resorts throughout the United Kingdom, proving herself to be a most sturdy and versatile vessel

The *Balmoral* in the King's Dock, Swansea, in 1993. Her green and cream hull and red funnel with a black top were one of a number of experimental colour schemes which were tried over the years. Some were popular, some were not! Eventually she reverted to her former Bristol Channel guise when she was painted in Campbells' colours, an arrangement which met with general approval.

The *Balmoral* in the former Charles Hill dry dock at Bristol in preparation for another season.

Above and below: The winter overhaul of the *Balmoral* relies heavily on voluntary labour. Members of the Paddle Steamer Preservation Society attend in force, especially at weekends, to ensure that the ship is turned out in pristine condition both above and below the waterline.

Above and below: The *Waverley* outward bound from Bristol to Ilfracombe.

The journey up and down the River Avon is one of the *Waverley*'s most popular excursions. It is, however, a difficult passage: the rapid tidal flow and the steep mudbanks call for precise timing and expert ship handling. The final three photographs in this volume illustrate the consummate skill and seamanship of the *Waverley*'s present master, Captain Graeme Gellatly, as he safely and surely negotiates the river's most difficult section, the Horseshoe Bend. In visiting the Port of Bristol, the *Waverley* sails, not only into the heart of the city, but also into the very core of its maritime history, upholding the enduring legacy and glorious tradition which Peter and Alexander Campbell began over a hundred years ago. Long may she continue to do so!